SERENIT

SERENITY

ISBN 978-1-77835-190-7

I wanted to put this book in sections but our minds and hearts are a mess never in order so this is how I'll let this book be.

To every lost soul…

Islam is the serenity that enters your
soul when it is left in a state of turmoil.

Eman Badawy

الا بذكر الله تطمئن القلوب (28)

Only in the remembrance of Allah do hearts find peace.

The ache in your heart is as temporary as the world that caused it.

Don’t chase the dunya when it was meant as a punishment for adam.

Lots of us claim to be muslim and believe in Allah and do the 5 pillars of Islam. We've come to a point where we think that's all what Islam is & that's all it comes to. we've made islam shallow for the majority forgetting the depth and beauty of it. Islam isn't just a label we claim its something we breath

“& be patient. surely, Allah is with those who are patient.” patience, in its true form, is one of the greatest acts of worship by being patient we are fully committing ourselves to the will of Allah n accepting whatever he may have written for us.

There is a certain kind of power that comes with fully accepting your circumstances for what it is. knowing that you can't change the situation in this immediate moment, but it doesn't mean that it will always be this way.

Say this to yourself when your sadness is overcoming your iman "Yes Allah, my heart hurts. & it might hurt for some time. But I know this is making me a stronger & better believer. I know behind every loss is a blessing, behind every fear is security, behind every hurt is healing, behind every painful tear is a beautiful smile awaiting to come up, and behind every dark phase is a beautiful daylight waiting to shine, all because behind every problem & hardship is your perfect planning & wisdom, your reasons and your decisions. & when I realize this, even in pain, I smile, even with tears rolling over, I know for sure, that you are enough for me, and your love is all that my broken heart needs."

Go to sleep tonight with no worries or thoughts of tomorrow and know that whatever happens Allah (SWT) has it taken care of

And surely with hardship comes ease.

My hijab is my shield during an active war.

Eman Badawy

He says walk to me and I'll run to you -
Hadith Qudsi

Billions of souls in the darkness and Allah chose yours to be guided by his mercy.

We say we have Islam as a priority and a value in life but what number priority is it? We put university and work before it, "I'll just pray later" we put our hangouts and friends before it "I'll cancel Quran class im busy I can attend next week". You delay wearing the hijab with the goal to wear it in uni or when you get married but who promised you tomorrow ? over & over again we come up with excuses excuses excuses and one day you'll stop. One day you're gonna go to sleep saying I'll pray Isha tomorrow and stay up to midnight so oversleep Fajr and you won't wake up in the morning. one day instead of waking up to good morning you'll wake up to " Who is your lord? What is your religion? Who is your prophet?"

Eman Badawy

Don't let go. Don't give up. And when you're all alone down to your realest layer remember that you have Allah (SWT) by your side.

Us humans complain a lot insanely about why Allah hasn't answered your dua as soon as you make it, or why he keeps testing you so much, but you forget his mercy of not punishing you right away when you sin.

Eman Badawy

When we cry we run to music instead of listening to the Quran, when we wanna rant and talk we facetime our friends instead of going in sujood to the one who calls you 5 times a day.

Eman Badawy

He loved you so he created hardship which made you return to him.

Prophet Muhammad صلى الله عليه وسلم said

“ Shall I not tell you who will be forbidden from the fire? every gentle, soft hearted and kind person” not a day I spend hating having a kind heart after that.

Allah (SWT) created us. He has the influence over people's hearts, so how can you believe he will keep you in the hearts of your loved ones after you took him out of yours?

Eman Badawy

Remember that " The crying of the sinners is more loved to Allah then the tasbeeh of the arrogant"

Islam scares people yet in islam we receive hasanat for simply smiling at one another.

Eman Badawy

A reminder your beauty is not defined by the views of others. It is not defined by how much body you're revealing or how much attention you're getting.

Eman Badawy

Why are we hopeless when our religion is full of hope. All the stories in the Quran have a happy ending so bear patience. Happy times will follow.

If creation is this beautiful like simple sunsets and pretty views then how much more then must it's creator be?

Eman Badawy

Allah himself has promised you with hardship comes ease, engrave these words in your heart and let it free you of stress. How can we cry & be worried with the promise of the greatest, most divine. Leave the worries, overthinking & stress behind you all that unnecessary negative thoughts when you have the creator of the planets & seven heavens by your side.

Eman Badawy

Let him love you and heal you and remind you that you are worthy.

Eman Badawy

If the universe didn't need you, you wouldn't be here.

Eman Badawy

Fall in love with him. he will hold you, he will protect you, he will care for you and he will ALWAYS be there for you

People say, I want someone to be there for me.
They forget that Allah is always there for us.
People say, I want someone to care for me.
They forget Allah cares even when we forget him.

ويحسبون كسر الروح هينًا وهو عند الله عظيم

- Ahmed Alsaer

" When you mention the sins of others their sins become yours" - Imam ali

I always thought that being a kind person was weakness until Islam taught me it's genuinely one of the purest and strongest thing you could ever be in life

Eman Badawy

When Allah wills to souls unite, no force on this earth can separate them

And do not let your depression or sad times let you lose your iman and tawakul in Allah, as for life comes with all emotions and tests some good and some bad

Fall in love with Allah and people will fall in love with you

Don't you cry over which has passed wallahi if there was any good in it, it would have stayed.

And in the depth of my heart breaks I found Allah

Eman Badawy

We don’t own our bodies they are simply amanah’s we have to take care of till they return to their owner. I know it’s hard to get out of bed sometimes but it's an obligation against you to take care of younger you.

Don't forget that our deen makes it an obligation to take care of ourselves and bodies.

Eman Badawy

I take hardship with a smile, the god of the seven skies thinks of me as strong

Eman Badawy

You keep wandering around trying to fill the hole in your heart, when will you realize only the prayer mat and your lord will fill it for you?

You can do it. No such thing as too many sins and
no such thing as a perfect human.
Go back to your lord. Don't delay start today.

Someone who truly loves you would care for your akhirah, not risk it. Wallahi don't be fooled

And do not be like those who forgot Allah so he made them forget themselves it is they who are truly rebellious

- Surah Al Hashr (19)

You don't know how much a simple kind act could change someone's day do it with pure intentions with no thought to how they would react

Eman Badawy

I made it a habit to listen to Quran before going to sleep Allah's words repeated to my soul all night with reassurance

Once you wear the hijab, you are formally representing islam in all of your actions. The hijab is an oath that you take when you wear it. The benefit of the hijab is that it allows you to wear islam publicly and to symbolize it before **anyone even meets you.**

وخيرة الله دومًا أجمل من أمانينا

God's goodness is always more beautiful
than our wishes

Reminder; ; Jannah is eternal

Abu Huraira reported: The messenger of Allah, peace and blessings be upon him, said;

“Whoever enters paradise will enjoy bliss without misery, clothes without wear, and youth without aging.”

He settles your matters while you drown in worry.

And what good does it do a person if he gains the world but loses himself?

Find enjoyment in the beautiful little things in life.

When you feel too weak just remember when you last felt the same but it passed

What runs down from the eye is not water, but a soul that's melted.

I'll wait because I know the first halal hug will make the years of wait disappear.

I fell in love with myself when I fell in love with islam

Maybe Allah isn't getting you the person that will complete half your deen yet, because he's waiting for you to fill your first half first.

Once you taste the sweetness of iman everything else becomes bitter.

@serenityserenity_

No heart has ever been torn after given to Allah

One dua is enough to get rid of a million sorrows

Appreciate the sacrifices our parents have made to give us the life they never had. Don't forget its their first time living too.

To the person reading this,
I hope soon you realize that everyone is going through their own battle after daylight,
that we drown in by the dims of the light.
So give kind words and be the light bulb in peoples lives.
And learn to give without expecting anything in return but the peace of your own mind.

Eman Badawy

How beautiful is it that a bunch of strangers with a million different lives gather next to each other to pray to one lord.

If you don't believe in your own abilities to achieve your goals, then believe in Allah's ability to help you

Eman Badawy

Peace in your heart starts when you say
" I trust you Allah"

Put Allah first and you will never be last

And do not question Allah’s tests perhaps he wants Jannah for you in replacement of the Dunya

Eman Badawy

The Quran is the manual book to life.

Eman Badawy

Treat people with manners without expecting and waiting for anything back.

He knows how you feel and he sees your pain and efforts. He knows the secret sorrows you hide
. Surah Baqarah {155-156}

And we will surely test you with something of fear and hunger and a loss of wealth and lives and fruits, but give good tidings to the patient,who, when disaster strikes them, say, “Indeed we belong to Allah, and indeed to him we will return.”

Oh the healer of the hearts guide my heart. And just as you keep the oceans apart from each other, keep me away from the punishment of hell and protect me of the tribulations of my grave.

He forgives us for sins we can’t forgive ourselves for.

Only Allah knows the tears hidden
behind your painful smile .

Don't ever turn cold when people don't give you the same warmth that you deserve.

Don't ever sell your deen for the validation of others and they will declare on judgment day "nafsi nafsi"

{37-34} وَلَا يَسْأَلُ حَمِيمٌ حَمِيمًا {34-37}

Carry islam proudly, you've got the creator of the universe by your side

Eman Badawy

Love in it's purest forms, loving the
divine without seeing him

Eman Badawy

How come we trust the pilot on the plane
without knowing him but can't trust
Allah to take care of us safely?

-Anonymous

Your past is your past it doesn't exist anymore

You can hide it from the world but Allah
knows what's inside of your heart

Eman Badawy

Wake up for tahajjud and take your lost soul to sujood

Eman Badawy

When the burdens of this dunya weigh heavily on you, drown your sorrows in sujood

The days which are the heaviest on your heart are also the days heaviest on your hasants scale

The most beautiful form of rizq is not
money rather it is, tranquility of a soul

Eman Badawy

Do not let the mouth that recites Quran recite swear words, do not let the eyes that read Allah's words watch sins and do not let the body we pray with, take part in zina.

Eman Badawy

I saw a quote that said
" Whenever you are alone, remind
yourself that Allah has sent everybody
away, so that it's only you and him."
and that hit beautifully

- Anonymous

A person on their deen will never hurt you.

He gave you so much when you didn't even
ask for anything. So now that you're
making dua what makes you think he's
gonna leave you empty handed

Eman Badawy

Islam is the protection of all the worldly harms. Proved by every sinner who got hurt with the income of the disobedience

Eman Badawy

Modesty is equally beautiful in men as it is in women. after all, the most modest of this ummah was Prophet Muhammad SAW

Heal before having children so your children don't have to heal for having you as a parent

Eman Badawy

Islam can make a woman so strong that she no longer strives to be noticed by men, no longer needs the admiring gaze to feel attractive, and no longer puts herself on display even though the entire world is doing just that.

Eman Badawy

Displaying yourself all over social media is not a trait a muslim should have. When you go to a jewelry store the best diamonds are saved covered inside for the special customers who enter the door and ask for it.

Eman Badawy

Surah Anfal : 70

“If Allah knows [any] good in your hearts, he will give you [something] better than what was taken from you, and he will forgive you; and allah is forgiving and merciful .”

When you fall, go into sujood.

Don’t mistake culture with deen

Haya is the beauty of a muslim, the guilt
we feel when we sin is a blessing once
you lose that you've lost yourself

Obtain the kindness of Abu bakr spent
his life salary to free his brothers and
sisters in islam despite not knowing them

Eman Badawy

There are things in life you haven't seen yet, things you haven't experienced yet that you are going to love when it gets to the time

Eman Badawy

Islam is the only deen that hasn't been changed from.

"فَبِأَيِّ آلاءِ رَبِّكُمَا تُكَذِّبَانِ"
{Surah Rahman}

Surround yourself with good people and watch how your manners and deen get better

One good action could be the reason why thousands of people make dua for you.

I am not a perfect muslim but I am not who I was 5 years ago. The love of Allah is so beautiful when you attain it, if there is a mountain falling behind you while you pray, you would not end the prayer because thats how much tawakkul and trust you have in Allah.

Forgive. Forgive the way you want Allah to forgive you. Throw that weight off you it's only harming you

"Attainment of inner peace is a direct reflection of the divine name the peace."

And there's still more to be found.

Message from the author

Serenity took days and nights to write, as a 16 year old I never imagined that one day I'd be publishing a book. I didn't know if it would be a success and that is not what I'm looking for, I figured if this book could help just one person, then it was worth it. I will publish it nonetheless. This book isn't all facts coming from the Quran rather what islam has made me believe in. With the best of intentions, I wrote this book so that others could learn the lessons I wish someone had shared with me while I was lost. In an effort to aid others in the same manner that I had wished to be assisted. I hope this book has given you a fresh perspective on how to approach life and opened your heart to new forms of love. Islam is an ongoing spiritual journey. Don't ever let it go for the temporary life pleasures and risk an eternity of Jannah. I hope by closing this book you got what you wanted when opening it.

Printed in Great Britain
by Amazon

46846510R00067